EMOTIONAL HEALTH ISSUES

Alcohol and Drug Abuse

Jillian Powell

WAYLAND

First published in 2008
by Wayland

Copyright © Wayland 2008

Wayland
338 Euston Road
London NW1 3BH

Wayland Australia
Level 17/207 Kent Street
Sydney, NSW 2000

Series editor: Nicola Edwards
Consultant: Peter Evans
Designer: Alix Wood
Picture researcher: Kathy Lockley

The case studies in this book are based on real experiences but the names we have used are fictitious and do not relate to real people. Except where a caption of a photograph specifically names a person appearing in that photograph, or an event in which real people have participated, all the people we have featured in the book are models.

The author and publisher would like to thank the following for allowing their pictures to be reproduced in this publication: Bubbles Photolibrary/Alamy: Cover, 12; Arben Celi/Reuters/Corbis: 34; D.R./Corbis Sygma: 29; Paul Doyle/Photofusion Picture Library: 38; Colin Edwards/Photofusion Picture Library: 33; Rick Gayle/Corbis: 14; Russell Glenister/image100/Corbis: 39; David Hoffman Photo Library/Alamy: 17, 28; Hutchings Stock Photography/Corbis: 32; Darrin Jenkins/Alamy: 7; Jupiterimages/FoodPix: 4; Lawrence Manning/Corbis: 11; James Marshall/Corbis: 18; Tom & Dee Ann McCarthy/Corbis: Title page, 20; Mediscan/Corbis: 6; Mira/Alamy: 40; MM Productions/Corbis: 44; Sonja Pacho/zefa/Corbis: 27; Pablo Paul/Alamy: 5; Jose Luis Pelaez, Inc/Corbis: 45; Jack Picone/Alamy: 16; Popperfoto/Alamy: 8; John Powell/Photofusion Picture Library: 13; James Quinton/Alamy: 36; Science Photo Library: 30; Alex Segre/Alamy: 23; Emma Smith/Photofusion Picture Library: 24; YM/epa/Corbis: 42

British Library Cataloguing in Publication Data

Powell, Jillian
    Alcohol and drug abuse. - (Emotional health issues)
    1. Alcorug abuse -
    Juvenile literature
    I. Title
    362.2'92'0835

ISBN: 978 0 7502 4913 3

Printed in China

Wayland is a division of Hachette Children's Books, an Hachette Livre UK company.

Contents

Words that appear in **bold** can be found in the
glossary on page 46.

Introduction

Megan is going to a club with her friends. It's what they do every Saturday night. First, they meet at her friend Chelsy's house so they can chat while they get ready. As they put on their makeup, they drink wine to relax and get in the party mood. When they get to the club, they usually have more wine and pints of beer. Megan knows she will probably have a hangover tomorrow, but she wants to enjoy herself tonight.

Megan is **binge drinking**. Binge drinking means drinking a large amount of alcohol in a short time – about three or four drinks within two hours. Binge drinking has become a common form of **alcohol abuse** among young people. Many young people use alcohol or cigarettes to relax when they are socialising and partying. Some use illegal drugs, such as Ecstasy, cannabis ('pot') and cocaine ('coke'), to make them feel relaxed or alert and to give them a feeling of **euphoria** – sometimes called a 'rush' or a 'high'. **Inhalants** and legal prescription and over-the-counter (OTC) medications can also be abused.

It is important to use alcohol responsibly. Many adults enjoy a glass of wine with a meal, and red wine may even carry some health benefits when drunk in moderation.

4

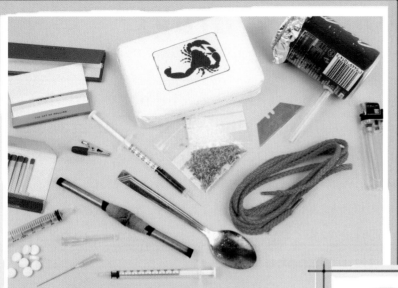

All these objects, from syringes to razor blades, cigarette papers and lighters, can be used by people to take illegal drugs.

What does alcohol and drug abuse mean?

People abuse alcohol or drugs when they drink or smoke or **ingest** substances in ways that can harm the mind or body. Binge drinking, smoking or chewing tobacco, and using recreational drugs can cause various health problems. They can lead to cancer, heart and liver disease, and can also give rise to serious mental and behavioural disorders.

Find out more

This book gives you the facts about alcohol and **drug abuse** and explains the effects those substances have on the brain and body. The book also deals with the reasons why young people are misusing alcohol and

It's a fact: drug use among young people

- Seven per cent of 13-year-olds have tried illegal drugs.
- One in ten teens has used illegal drugs.
- Around 65 per cent of children have tried cigarettes.
- Among 16- to 24-year-olds, one in two young people, has tried illegal drugs.

drugs. You will find advice on how to seek help in overcoming **addiction**. You will also learn that it is possible to have a fun social life and relax without using drugs or alcohol.

Chapter 1: *What are drugs?*

Drugs are substances that affect the way the body and the brain function. Many different kinds of drugs affect the body in different ways. They include legal drugs such as the caffeine in coffee and the nicotine in tobacco, as well as illegal or 'classified' drugs such as cannabis, Ecstasy, cocaine and heroin. All drugs, legal or illegal, can be dangerous, and some are addictive and can create drug **dependency**.

Why do people take drugs?

People take drugs for different reasons. Many take medicines that their doctors have prescribed for health reasons. Some people believe that drinking a moderate amount of alcohol carries some health benefits. Some recent studies have provided evidence that drinking moderate amounts of wine, beer, or other alcoholic beverages (with two or three 'alcohol-free' days during each week) may be good for the heart and may reduce the risk of **Alzheimer's** and other diseases. Some people take drugs for 'recreational' purposes – that is, to relax or stimulate them or to give them a feeling of euphoria.

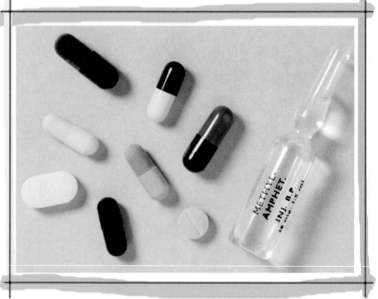

Some drugs can legally be bought 'over the counter', but can be addictive if taken long term.

Legal drugs

Legal drugs include alcohol, cigarettes, and OTC painkillers. Other legal drugs have to be prescribed by a doctor, and obtained from a pharmacy with a

Illegal drugs

Illegal drugs fall into different classes or categories. The most harmful class includes heroin, cocaine, Ecstasy and LSD. The next class includes amphetamines, (sometimes called 'speed') and **barbiturates**, (sometimes called 'downers'). The next covers drugs including cannabis, tranquillizers and **anabolic steroids**.

Each class carries different penalties for possessing, supplying or trafficking in them, ranging from fines to long imprisonment. All the above drugs are illegal for children and teens under 18 apart from those that are prescribed by doctors. Shopkeepers are not allowed to sell cigarettes or alcohol to under-age teens.

prescription. Some people abuse legal drugs such as tranquillizers, painkillers, **sedatives** and **amphetamines**, by using them for recreational, not medical, purposes. Many of these drugs can be addictive if taken long term.

Crack cocaine is one of the most harmful and addictive illegal drugs. Users smoke it, which means large amounts of it reach their brains very rapidly.

Recreational drugs

People have used drugs for recreational purposes for thousands of years. Recreational drugs include alcohol, caffeine, tobacco and cannabis. Native Americans smoked tobacco, and the Aztecs of Mexico used 'magic mushrooms' (mushrooms that contain the drugs psilocin and psilocybin) during religious ceremonies.

In Asia, opium (from the opium poppy) and cannabis have a long history of use for relaxation. Some native peoples of the Andes in South America chew coca leaves, which contain cocaine, to boost their energy levels and help with **altitude sickness**. In Africa and the Middle East, **khat** is used in the same way.

The 'flower power' culture of the 1960s encouraged the use of drugs such as cannabis and magic mushrooms.

Drug trends

Cannabis began to gain popularity in the West in the 1950s, then became very popular during the 1960s. By the 1980s, drugs such as cocaine and Ecstasy emerged as favourite club drugs. More recently, there has been a rise in the use of 'crack' cocaine (see page 7), a highly addictive form of cocaine that can be smoked, and crystal methamphetamine, a **stimulant** that can be snorted (inhaled through the nose), injected or smoked as 'ice'.

Gamma hydroxybutyric acid (or GHB, a liquid form of Ecstasy), which is used by some bodybuilders to stimulate muscle growth, is also used in clubs for its euphoric effects. A dangerous trend is 'speedballing', or combining crack cocaine with heroin.

Inhalants

More young people are also using inhalant drugs, an extremely dangerous practice. Inhalant drugs are substances sold legally for other purposes, including **solvents** (nail polish removers, marker pens and glue) gases (aerosols, spray paints) and **nitrites** (room deodorizers). They give off strong chemical vapours that are inhaled as mind-altering drugs. They can either be inhaled by 'huffing' – sniffing or snorting them direct from containers – or by 'bagging', which means inhaling them from inside a plastic or paper bag.

Taking risks

Sometimes, being depressed can drive people to take serious risks. Depressed teenagers may start abusing drugs or drinking large amounts of alcohol. They may shoplift, drive recklessly, or engage in unsafe sexual practices. Their risky behaviour is a sign that they are feeling desperate. Without any hope for the future, they simply don't care what happens to them. High-risk behaviour can also be a cry for help.

Prescription drugs

Another form of drug abuse is using prescription drugs for recreational purposes. The drug methylphenidate (one brand name is Ritalin) is prescribed for children with attention-deficit/hyperactivity disorder (ADHD) to improve concentration, but some young people use it illegally as a 'diet

pill' or as a stimulant when cramming for tests. In the United States, there is a growing trend for young people to crush and snort or inject painkilling drugs such as hydrocodone and oxycodone to give them a sudden 'rush' or 'high'. Recently, there has been an increase in the use of clenbuterol, a drug prescribed to treat asthma in horses, as a weight-loss pill.

Some people obtain drugs by prescription and then illegally sell the medications to others. Drugs can also be obtained through online pharmacies without a prescription, making them more easily available to young people.

It's a fact: cannabis, amphetamines and inhalants

- Cannabis is the most widely used illegal drug.
- One in five 15-year-olds smokes cannabis regularly.
- Eight per cent of teens have used amphetamines.
- One in seven 15- to16-year-olds uses inhalants.

Chapter 2: *How drugs and alcohol affect the body*

Drugs can be swallowed, smoked, inhaled through the nose or mouth, or injected into the blood. Whichever method is used, drugs get into the bloodstream, which carries them to the brain and other parts of the body. They dock on to **receptors** in the brain and change the ways nerve cells communicate. Different drugs act on different areas of the brain, altering the balance of brain chemicals. These changes cause the feelings associated with drug taking, such as euphoria and relaxation.

Stimulants and depressants

Stimulants such as cocaine send 'fake' messages from the brain telling the body that it is under stress. As a result, heart rate and blood pressure increase. Stimulants also cause a build-up of the 'reward' chemical **dopamine** in the brain, giving a feeling of euphoria. Blood to the skin reduces, so the body is less able to cool down, and body temperature can rise rapidly.

Depressants include GHB and alcohol. They slow down messages between the brain and body. Reactions, heart rate and breathing slow down, giving a feeling of relaxation.

Hallucinogens

Hallucinogens include Ecstasy and LSD. They increase heart rate, blood pressure and body temperature. Hallucinogens affect the parts of the brain that control mood, perception and sensory signals. These drugs can distort the way people see, hear or feel things, confusing the senses and causing vivid dreamlike experiences.

Inhalants

Inhalants include solvents, gases and nitrites. When inhaled, they can have mind-altering effects, leading to feelings of euphoria and giddiness. They can also cause rapid or irregular heartbeat, a fall in blood pressure and

The club and rave culture that began in the 1980s encouraged the use of drugs such as Ecstasy. Clubbers took Ecstasy as it helped them to stay awake and dance all night long.

other symptoms including nausea and vomiting. If they build up in the lungs, depriving the body of oxygen, they can cause breathing failure. Some solvent sprays can freeze the **larynx** and lungs, resulting in suffocation.

CASE STUDY

Jamie had never used drugs until a friend offered him Ecstasy at a concert. Jamie found that the 'hug drug' made him very talkative, and he felt that everyone around him was his friend. He started taking Ecstasy every other weekend, then every weekend. Soon he was taking it four or five times a week. At parties he began taking more than one pill, sometimes forgetting how many he had taken. On his 17th birthday, he went to a club with his friends and took three 'hits' of Ecstasy. He was dancing when he suddenly became very hot and sweaty. His heart started racing, and he collapsed, unable to lift his head off the ground. His body was overheating. Jamie was rushed to a hospital in an ambulance for emergency treatment.

What happens when someone drinks alcohol?

Alcohol is a depressant drug. It depresses the central nervous system, slowing communication between nerve cells in the brain and other cells.

When a person drinks alcohol, it passes into the stomach and small intestine. About 20 per cent of the alcohol is absorbed in the stomach and the rest is absorbed in the small intestine. From there, alcohol passes through small blood vessels into the bloodstream, which carries the alcohol to the brain and other organs.

Processing alcohol

Once alcohol is in the bloodstream, the body processes it in three ways. About 5 per cent goes through the kidneys and is passed as urine. Another 5 per cent is exhaled in the breath (this is detectable by a Breathalyser device). The rest is broken down by

Lager is a popular drink among teens, particularly boys. Different lagers vary in strength and sometimes the alcoholic content of a small amount of lager is high enough to raise blood alcohol concentration rapidly.

enzymes in the liver into acetic acid. The rate at which alcohol is absorbed in the body is affected by many different factors. They include the drinker's weight, sex and **metabolism**, the amount and strength of alcohol drunk, the type of drink (fizzy drinks tend to be absorbed faster) and the type and amount of food eaten. Food (especially fats and fruit sugars) is known to dilute alcohol and slow down the rate at which it is absorbed.

Blood alcohol concentration

The liver processes one alcoholic drink (or about 14 grams of alcohol) in about one hour. If someone drinks more than that amount in an hour, alcohol is stored in the bloodstream, raising the **blood alcohol concentration (BAC)**. BAC measures

Alcohol poisoning

Within eight to 12 hours of heavy drinking, drinkers can feel effects that include shakiness, extreme thirst, nausea, headache and fatigue. A hangover is a combination of **withdrawal** symptoms and mild **alcohol poisoning**. If BAC rises above 0.30 per cent, alcohol poisoning can lead to loss of consciousness and coma; at about 0.40 per cent, death can result.

the ratio of alcohol in the bloodstream. BAC can rise within 20 minutes of drinking alcohol. As BAC rises, alcohol begins to act on nerve cells in the brain, affecting the drinker's feelings and behaviour. As different areas of the brain are affected, the drinker typically goes through a sequence of feelings that include euphoria and relaxation, sleepiness, loss of balance and coordination, confusion, dizziness and aggression.

In focus: women and alcohol

Women tend to feel the effects of alcohol more than men, even if they are the same weight. This is because women have less water (52 per cent) in their bodies than men (61 per cent) to dilute alcohol. Women also have smaller amounts of the liver enzymes that break down alcohol. Their monthly hormonal cycles can also affect the rate at which alcohol is absorbed.

What happens when someone smokes?

Cigarettes contain approximately 4000 different chemicals, including nicotine, tar and carbon monoxide. Nicotine is a highly addictive drug found in tobacco.

Effects of smoke

Within seconds of taking the first puff on a cigarette, irritating gases start working on the **membranes** of the eyes, nose and throat. In time, this irritation can lead to a 'smoker's cough'. Cigarette smoke also dries the skin and narrows the blood vessels

Smokers inhale a cocktail of chemicals every time they draw on a cigarette. The smoke from a cigarette can damage the health of people who breathe it in, too.

inside it, reducing blood flow and ageing the appearance of the smoker's skin.

Inhaling

As a smoker inhales, the gases irritate the lungs and airways, encouraging them to make mucous. As the smoke reaches the lungs, the heart has to work harder. A person's heart rate can increase by up to 30 per cent during the first ten minutes of smoking. Tar in the smoke condenses, and about 70 per cent is deposited in the lungs. Condensed tar can also stain a smoker's teeth and fingers yellow. Carbon monoxide and other gases pass from the lungs into the bloodstream.

Carbon monoxide is a deadly gas that is also found in car exhaust fumes. It slows down oxygen-carrying cells in the blood, reducing the amount of oxygen that reaches the brain and muscles.

Nicotine

It takes fewer than ten seconds for nicotine to pass from the lungs into the bloodstream and from there to the smoker's brain. When the brain detects nicotine it triggers the release of the hormone adrenaline, which stimulates the central nervous system. This sends messages to tighten the blood vessels and make the blood more sticky, increasing the smoker's heart and breathing rates and blood pressure. As a result, the heart has to work harder to pump blood throughout the body.

Nicotine then docks on to chemical receptors in the smoker's brain, increasing levels of enzymes that boost the 'reward' chemical dopamine. Dopamine stimulates brain cells, enhancing mood and energy. It is responsible for the 'high' that keeps smokers addicted to cigarettes.

The effect of nicotine lasts from around 40 minutes to two hours. As the body becomes tolerant of nicotine, a person needs to smoke more cigarettes to achieve the same effect of stimulation or relaxation.

In focus: smoking and diets

Smoking increases the rate at which the body burns calories, and nicotine can also suppress appetite. This can tempt some girls to take up smoking as a weight-loss aid. But smoking is always harmful to health, and it alters the way fat is distributed in the body. Smokers tend to carry more fat around the waist and upper body, increasing their risk of heart and other diseases.

What is addiction?

Some drugs are addictive. This means that drug users may develop a dependency or addiction to them that makes them go on using them. Addiction can be physical and/or psychological.

Physical dependency

Some drugs, including nicotine, alcohol and heroin, cause physical dependency. They do this by reinforcing reward pathways in the brain. These drugs stimulate pleasure-giving chemicals such as dopamine and **endorphins**, so the drug user feels good and wants to take the drugs again to get the same feeling of pleasure. When a person becomes physically addicted to a drug, the body reacts with a feeling of loss and uncomfortable or painful physical sensations if the person stops taking the drug. Withdrawal symptoms can range from anxiety and irritation to tremors, convulsions and pain.

The physical symptoms caused by withdrawal from drugs are known as 'doing cold turkey'. The symptoms vary in intensity and duration depending on the type of drug the user has been taking.

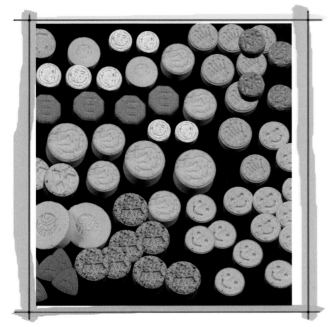

'Tabs' of Ecstasy come in different forms and colours. They often have a picture such as a smiley face stamped on them.

Withdrawal from alcohol and other depressants can even result in death.

Psychological dependency

Drugs such as cocaine and amphetamines do not cause physical dependency, but they do cause strong psychological dependency. This dependency can last much longer, for years or even for a lifetime. It comes from the memory of pleasure associated with the drug. The drug user has an intense desire, or craving, to take the drug to feel the same pleasure again.

People who are psychologically addicted to a drug feel they have to go on using it, even though they know drug abuse is harming their health and their life. They may fear the pain of withdrawal. Sometimes, they associate certain people or places with taking the drug, so their environment can trigger their craving.

Drug tolerance

When someone takes a drug regularly, the body can develop a **tolerance** to it. Receptors in the brain become adapted to the drug, so that the person must use more and more of the substance to get the same sensations of pleasure, stimulation or relaxation.

As with alcohol, increasing tolerance to a drug encourages users to move to stronger drugs, or to take larger or more frequent doses.

In focus: is there an addiction gene?

Some studies have shown that people who are impulsive may be more likely to become addicted to drugs. Some scientists believe that there may be a *gene* that reduces the number of dopamine receptors in the brain. People with fewer dopamine receptors may be more likely to become addicted to the pleasure-giving effects of drugs.

Chapter 3: *A growing problem*

People are starting to smoke and take illegal drugs at younger ages than ever before. The younger people are when they begin to smoke, the more likely they are to become addicted to nicotine. Most smokers begin using tobacco in their teens. By the age of 15, one in six boys and one in four girls are regular smokers. They might have been given cigarettes by siblings or friends who smoke. They might have bought them illegally. About half of all under-age children who attempt to buy cigarettes succeed in doing so.

Illegal drugs

Recent surveys show that children as young as nine or ten have tried drugs such as inhalants, cannabis, and Ecstasy. Some youngsters are offered drugs at the playground, in school, or at parties. The number of children and teens inhaling household substances such as cleaning fluids is also rising. Household products are easily available, which may account for the increase in their use among young children. They are sometimes wrongly seen as less harmful than other drugs, although in fact they are highly dangerous, and can lead to breathing failure, suffocation and sudden death.

Young people may start experimenting with drugs such as inhalants and then move on to try others. It takes just days for a tolerance of inhalants to build up.

Risky behaviour

A growing number of young people are experimenting with combinations of drugs. Some take drugs at the same time as drinking alcohol. Others take stimulants like Ritalin at the same time as inhaling solvents such as room deodorizers or correction fluids. This can disturb the heart rhythm, and it increases the risk of health problems and even death.

Speedballing is the practice of injecting heroin and crack cocaine together. Some dealers sell them as a package, or offer the cocaine for free to encourage use. The combined effect of taking a stimulant and depressant drug increases the 'rush' but there is a greater risk of overdosing. Speedballers also tend to inject drugs more frequently and are more likely to share needles, increasing the risk of blood infections and diseases like HIV. Combining any drugs, including alcohol, greatly increases the risk of overdose and health problems.

It's a fact: smoking

- Every day, 450 children in the UK and more than 3,000 people between the ages of 12 and 17 in the United States begin smoking cigarettes.
- Four out of five smokers start in their teens.
- Ninety per cent of teen smokers are addicted by the age of 18.
- Worldwide, about one in five 13- to 15-year-olds smokes.
- Children of smokers are more than twice as likely to smoke as children of parents who do not smoke.

CASE STUDY

Bethany and her friends tried inhaling nail polish one night because they thought it would be a laugh. Bethany had never bought illegal drugs but inhaling gave her a giddy feeling and when she was alone she started experimenting with inhaling different solvents like marker pens and hair spray. It felt like a way of forgetting about exam stress and problems at home since her dad had left. One night she got talking to others in a chat room online and they encouraged her to experiment with bagging. The next day, her mother found her collapsed in her room. Bethany had passed out after breathing in toxic fumes from a bag. She had to be rushed to hospital.

Under-age drinking

Children are drinking alcohol at increasingly young ages, resulting in poor performance and accidents in school. In the UK, for example, surveys show that nearly one in five 11- to 15-year-olds drinks alcohol at least once a week. Thousands of 11- to 15- year-olds need treatment each year for alcohol poisoning or mental or behavioural problems resulting from heavy drinking. There are reports of children as young as eight or nine being hospitalised after drinking alcohol.

Children are also drinking alcohol more frequently and in larger amounts than ever before. Studies show that children are drinking twice as much alcohol today as they were in 1990. Some people believe that '**alco pops**' have encouraged this trend. These are

Young people often look to alcohol and other drugs such as cannabis to relax them and give them a feeling of confidence socially.

ready-mixed drinks that have a sweet taste but contain up to 5 per cent alcohol – the same as a strong lager. Alco pops are particularly popular with girls. Boys are more likely to drink beer, cider and lager. Many under-15s drink too much alcohol; some drink as many as five bottles of alco pops or five pints of cider a week.

Binge drinking

Binge drinking (see page 4) is a growing problem among teens, especially girls. The 'ladette' culture – girls behaving like lads – has encouraged heavy drinking among girls. According to recent surveys in the UK, nearly one in three girls and one in four boys aged 15 to 16 admitted to binge drinking more than once in the previous month.

Some teenagers say that they drink alcohol to get drunk. They combine beer with spirits such as vodka to get drunk as quickly as possible. They say drinking makes them lose their inhibitions as they dance or talk at parties or in other social settings.

Young people who are not used to the effects of drinking alcohol may drink it as though they are consuming soft drinks and then find that they become very ill as a result. They may even end up being admitted to hospital with alcohol poisoning.

CASE STUDY

Like most people at her college, Amy went out with her friends every weekend. She never thought of herself as a binge drinker, just as someone who enjoyed drinking socially. She had never used other drugs and she thought of alcohol as a safe way to unwind and have fun. Alcohol made her much more talkative and relaxed, and when she was drinking she found that she could forget about her coursework and everyday worries.

When she went out, she typically drank a few beers, a double vodka and coke and two or three glasses of wine. In a single night, Amy consumed the maximum number of recommended units of alcohol *per week* for a woman. Over the course of a week, she drank enough alcohol to cause liver damage in the long term.

Young people who get themselves into a drunken state on a night out put themselves at all sorts of risk. They are more likely to have an accident on the way home or when they get home. For example, half of all the pedestrians who are killed on the road have been drinking alcohol and around half of all household fires are drink related.

Chapter 4: Why do young people use alcohol and drugs?

What makes children and teens start smoking or drinking, or taking other drugs? There are many different reasons, including the availability of cigarettes, alcohol and other drugs, **peer pressure**, and a desire to rebel. Many young people are aware of the health risks they are taking, but choose to ignore them. Influences around them can encourage them to ignore or deny the risks.

Availability

Although shops are not allowed to sell alcohol or cigarettes to under-age children, many young people are able to buy them before they reach the minimum legal age. They may also persuade older friends or siblings to buy them for them. Drugs such as cannabis have become increasingly widely available as a result of dealers targeting children in schools and clubs and on the street.

Peer pressure

Peer pressure means the influence that friends of the same age have on a person. Children and teens have a natural feeling of wanting

CASE STUDY

Daniel had his first cigarette when he was 11. He was feeling really stressed about exams, and his friend Craig told him that smoking would calm him down. Daniel refused at first because his granddad had died from lung cancer. Craig said Daniel was just being stupid and started making fun of him in front of their other friends at school. Craig said Daniel was a baby for refusing to smoke. Daniel went home and secretly took one of his mum's cigarettes. He wanted to know what it was like to smoke. He also wanted to try it out on his own, without Craig and the others around. Daniel felt quite pleased with himself when he found he could inhale without coughing. The next time Craig and the others were smoking, he asked them for a cigarette. He smoked it with them and felt like a part of the crowd.

For some young girls, cigarettes and alcohol can seem a vital part of a 'good night out'. Alcohol can make people who drink it feel relaxed and sociable, but heavy drinking can cause both short- and long-term harm.

to belong and be accepted by their peers. Many are persuaded to try cigarettes, alcohol or drugs because their friends suggest it is a cool thing to do. If they say no, they run the risk of their peers making fun of them or bullying them and excluding them from their group. Girls may also take up smoking because they think it will help them stay slim or lose weight.

Desire to rebel

It is not uncommon for teens to want to rebel against the values of older people, whether they are parents, teachers or the government. Young people naturally feel the need to state ownership of their own minds and bodies. They feel they have the right to decide what they can do, and what risks they can take. They can also feel immune to health risks because they are young and the problems of middle or old age seem a very long way off.

Influences on young people

Children whose parents or siblings smoke, drink or use other drugs are more likely to start the habit themselves. This behaviour has been 'normalised' by the people around them. Children and teens are also influenced by the fictional characters they see on television and in films. Celebrities such as singers, actors and models can be powerful role models for teens. Stars who smoke, drink and take drugs may convince young people that those ways of behaving are acceptable and even desirable.

A genetic link?

Some scientists believe that people's genes may influence their drinking habits. Researchers have found evidence that genetic makeup can affect the likeliness of developing an addiction to alcohol or other drugs. Certain genes may produce changes in

If young people see family members turning to alcohol as a means of coping with problems, they may feel encouraged to copy them.

the brain that make a person more sensitive to the effects of drugs. Scientists have identified a particular gene that controls chemical signalling in the brain that may influence the 'high' some people get from drugs. Certain genes may also make people more impulsive and more likely to take risks.

Advertising and sponsorship

Children and teens are bombarded with images of alcohol through advertising. These adverts deliberately target the young by showing scenes at clubs, concerts and sports events. Adverts often feature content that is known to appeal to children and teens, such as humour, music or celebrities. Studies show that even young children are aware of alcohol advertisements and remember them.

Advertising rules have recently been toughened to ban adverts targeting the under-18s, but many people have called for a total ban on advertising alcohol before the 9 pm 'watershed'. Alcohol adverts are already banned

In focus: targeting young people

The alcohol industry is continually developing new products aimed at particular consumer groups such as teens or young women. Alco pops, introduced in the 1990s, were aimed specifically at young drinkers, especially girls. These ready-mixed drinks are brightly coloured, with a sweet, fruit juice taste.

Recently new herbal drinks containing vodka, fruit and Chinese herbs have been launched. The advertisements for these drinks link them with the idea that people who drink them feel sexier and more attractive to others.

from being shown during programmes for which more than 20 per cent of the audience are children.

The alcohol industry also targets teens by sponsoring sports teams and contests and music events. The companies appeal to teens with websites that offer interactive games, competitions, accessories, chat rooms and screensavers. In the UK, laws have recently been introduced banning alcohol companies from advertising on products marketed to children, such as replica sports shirts.

Chapter 5: *Health costs*

Scientists have found that drinking alcohol can harm young brains. They believe it damages the brain's learning powers and leads to memory problems later in life. Doctors say that drinking alcohol can cause emotional and behavioural problems and make young people more likely to become addicted to alcohol when they are older. Binge drinking is especially harmful and may affect the way in which a young person's nervous and reproductive systems develop.

Alcohol-related diseases

Heavy drinking puts a strain on the liver, heart, pancreas and other organs. It can raise blood pressure, increasing the risk of strokes and heart attacks. It also damages the red muscle fibres needed for stamina in sport. In time, it can lead to serious diseases including **cirrhosis** of the liver, heart disease, cancer and **osteoporosis**.

Drinking in pregnancy

If a woman drinks alcohol during pregnancy, her unborn child is at risk of health problems. Even small amounts of alcohol can cause birth defects and damage the baby's

It's a fact: drinking alcohol

- Alcohol is high in calories and has no real nutritional value.
- Heavy drinking can contribute to weight problems and **obesity**.
- Alcohol can dehydrate the body, leading to early skin ageing.
- Acidic drinks such as wine and alco pops can damage tooth enamel.
- Heavy drinking makes people more accident-prone and increases the likelihood that they will engage in risky behaviour.
- 'Date rape' has been linked to alcoholic drinks spiked with drugs such as GHB (liquid Ecstasy).

Alcohol can make girls more likely to risk having unsafe sex, and drinks can also be spiked with 'date rape' drugs.

developing nervous system. It can also lead to a lifetime of behavioural and learning difficulties. **Foetal Alcohol Syndrome** (FAS) is the most common cause of non-genetic learning disabilities in the West, and one that is 100 per cent preventable. A 20-year-old born with FAS will have the emotional maturity of a 6-year-old. He or she may also have abnormal facial features or other body parts.

In focus: the liver and alcohol

Liver disease (cirrhosis) was once found mainly in older men. But recently it has risen by a third in young women due to regular heavy or binge drinking.

Cirrhosis means that normal liver tissue is replaced by scar tissue. This blocks the flow of blood through the liver and makes it unable to process toxins properly.

Women are more likely to suffer liver damage because their bodies are lighter than men's and have a different ratio of fat to water. Body metabolism and hormones can also play a part.

Drugs and health

Some scientists believe that drugs may lead to mental health problems including depression and **paranoia**. Their studies show that some drugs may do long-term harm to the brain. This is more likely with regular or heavy drug use. They also believe that brains are more likely to be harmed during adolescence, when they are still developing.

Cannabis

Studies show that cannabis can cause long-term chemical changes in the brain and make users more likely to try other drugs. Half the people who use cannabis suffer paranoia, panic attacks and blackouts. Young people who use cannabis regularly or heavily can have problems including mood swings, poor motivation and sickness. They are twice as likely to develop **psychosis**. This type of mental illness includes conditions such as **schizophrenia**. Cannabis increases levels of the 'pleasure' chemical dopamine in the brain, but too much dopamine can cause psychosis. There are different varieties of cannabis, of varying strengths (see the focus box opposite).

Ecstasy

During adolescence, the dopamine receptors in the brain are changing and developing. Studies suggest that using cannabis, cocaine or amphetamines may alter the receptors permanently. Even small amounts of Ecstasy may harm first-time users by decreasing blood flow to the brain. Loss of concentration and memory can result. Long-term use may

The dried leaves of the cannabis plant (seen at the top of this photo) are known as grass. Lumps of cannabis resin (shown in the centre of the photo) are called hash. Cannabis is commonly mixed with tobacco and smoked as 'spliffs' or 'joints'.

'Crack' cocaine gets its name from the crackling sound it makes when it is heated. Crack can be smoked or made into a solution and injected into the user's body.

damage the brain cells that make **serotonin**, leading to depression, anxiety and sleep problems.

Cocaine and heroin

When people take drugs in childhood or in their teens, they are more likely to become addicted. Drugs such as cocaine and heroin can take over lives, making regular users desperate to get hold of more. Snorting cocaine can damage and even destroy tissue in and around the nose. Injecting drugs such as heroin carries other risks, including overdosing and passing on infections including hepatitis C, HIV and Aids.

In danger of dying

In some cases, taking drugs leads to death. This can be caused by contaminated drugs, an allergic reaction or 'water intoxication'. This happens when a young person drinks too much water after taking drugs. The drugs prevent the body processing water in the normal way, so body tissues swell, leading to fits, **coma** and even death.

In focus: *skunk cannabis*

The active ingredient in cannabis is THC (tetrahydrocannabinol). In the 1960s when cannabis first became a popular 'party' drug, it contained between 2 and 4 per cent of THC. But today's 'skunk' varieties are much stronger, containing between 10 and15 per cent. Most cannabis users move on to stronger varieties as they become addicted.

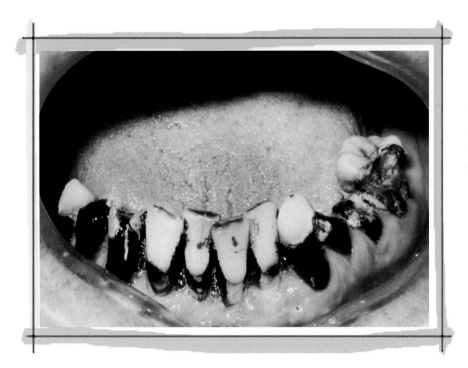

This smoker's teeth have been stained black by the tar in cigarettes.

Tobacco and health

Smoking harms health and fitness in many ways. Children who smoke are more likely to suffer coughs, wheezing and other breathing problems. If they smoke regularly, they are four times more likely to develop asthma during their teenage years. Smoking also damages the **cilia** that keep germs out of the throat, so children who smoke are more likely to suffer colds and other infections.

Smoking reduces fitness and energy levels. It stains teeth and fingers yellow and makes the breath smell bad. Children who smoke are also more likely to experiment with other drugs.

Smoking-related diseases

The younger children are when they start smoking, the more likely they are to become addicted to nicotine and die early from smoking-related diseases. More people die from heart and lung diseases caused by tobacco than any other drug.

Cigarettes contain a poisonous mix of gases, tar and chemicals, including the addictive drug nicotine. The presence of nicotine in the body puts a strain on the heart (see page 15), increasing the risk of heart disease and strokes. Carbon monoxide prevents blood carrying enough oxygen to the brain and muscles. Tar clogs up the lungs and contains cancer-causing chemicals.

Studies show that these chemicals damage the DNA of the lungs. The highest levels of damage to DNA have been found in smokers aged between the ages of 9 and 12.

Chewing smokeless or 'spit' tobacco is also harmful to the body. It leads to nicotine addiction, and can cause heart disease and mouth, gum and other cancers.

Second-hand smoke

Passive smoking (breathing in someone else's cigarette smoke) is also harmful to health, especially for babies and children. This may be because their lungs are still developing, and they breathe faster than adults, so they inhale more smoke.

If a woman smokes during her pregnancy, this can harm the baby, and lead to low birth weight, premature birth and even miscarriage. It also increases the risk of the child developing cancer in later life.

Countries including Ireland and the UK as well as some states in the US, have recently banned smoking in public places such as clubs, bars and restaurants. Campaign groups had been calling for a ban, to protect the health of staff who have to work in smoky environments.

CASE STUDY

Nicola started smoking when she was twelve. By the age of 17 she was smoking 20 cigarettes a day. When her sister, who was also a smoker, became pregnant, Nicola went with her to her appointments at the antenatal clinic. A nurse at the clinic explained how smoking could damage the baby in the womb, and how passive smoking harmed babies and children. Nicola's sister decided to take the nurse's advice to join a smokers' clinic to help her quit and Nicola decided to stop smoking too to support her sister.

Each week at the clinic they checked carbon monoxide levels in Nicola's sister's blood. Nicola could see that when her sister stopped smoking, there was no carbon monoxide in her blood, which meant her baby was getting more oxygen. With the help of the clinic, she managed to stop smoking and her baby was born with a healthy birth weight. Nicola saved the money she would have spent on cigarettes and put it towards clothes and toys for her sister's new baby.

Chapter 6: *Social costs*

Alcohol is responsible for many kinds of crime, including drink driving. Even drinking a small amount of alcohol increases the chance of having a road accident. But in spite of strict laws and advertising campaigns warning of the dangers, cases of drink driving have risen in the past decade. Young people between the ages of 17 and 24 are most likely to drink drive. According to some surveys, more than one in four young people are still drink driving, and there have been cases of children as young as 12 drink driving. Road accidents related to alcohol are now the leading cause of death among young people.

Crime and violence

According to recent figures, alcohol causes nearly half of all violent crime and up to a third of all crimes worldwide. Most violent crime happens between 9 pm and 3 am when pubs and clubs close, and many city and town centres have become 'no go' areas at night because of widespread drunk and disorderly behaviour and criminal damage. Alcohol is behind more than three-quarters of all assaults and nearly 90 per cent of criminal damage cases.

Police have stopped a driver on suspicion of drink driving. He has been asked to walk along a straight line to indicate if he is under the influence of alcohol.

In the UK, it is linked to one in four cases of violence in the home, and rates of domestic violence rise after heavy drinking following important football matches.

Tens of thousands of people each year are cautioned or found guilty of offences of drunkenness. The majority are in their teens. Teens who drink heavily are more likely to get involved in crimes such as shoplifting and vandalism.

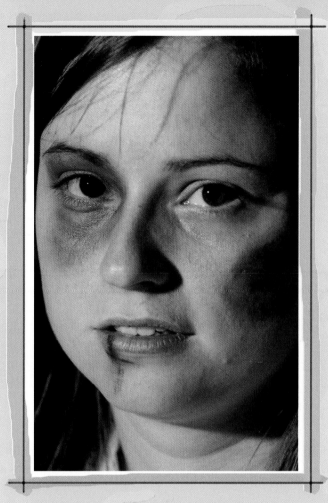

Many women who report incidents of domestic violence tell the police that their partner had been under the influence of alcohol when the abuse occurred.

It's a fact: alcohol and crime

- Almost 600 people are killed in drink driving accidents each year.
- Alcohol is a factor in about a third of all police arrests.
- Alcohol is behind 70 per cent of admissions to hospital accident and emergency wards at weekends.
- An estimated 20 to 30 per cent of crimes and accidents worldwide are related to alcohol.

Risks and dangers

Alcohol abuse has been linked with deaths by drowning, suicide and murder. In the United States, six young people die every day from suicide or murder linked to alcohol abuse. Young people who drink heavily are also more likely to be the victim of violent attacks, rape and theft.

Sniffer dogs are used at airports to foil attempts to smuggle drugs into countries. The dogs are trained to sniff out illegal drugs that have been hidden in luggage.

Drugs and crime

Young people who abuse drugs can get into trouble at home, at school, with their friends and with the police. They are more likely to have accidents and to commit crime. Taking drugs regularly can be an expensive habit that results in debt. People who become addicted may commit crimes, including shoplifting, to get money to buy drugs. They may become dealers and sell drugs to others. Some dealers recruit children as 'look outs' or drug runners. They sometimes give out 'free samples' of drugs in schools or clubs to encourage new users.

Possessing and supplying drugs

It is illegal to possess or supply classified drugs and anyone caught may be fined or imprisoned. Supply can mean dealing in drugs, or buying drugs to share with others, or offering to share them. It is also illegal to sell on drugs prescribed by a doctor. Yet recent surveys have found young people are selling prescribed drugs to others for recreational use. The drug

Ritalin, prescribed to children with ADHD, is being sold in school playgrounds for use as a stimulant or an appetite suppressant to aid weight loss. Prescription drugs can be addictive, and it is dangerous for anyone to take drugs that a doctor has prescribed for someone else.

Drugs and driving

It is illegal to drive after taking drugs as they can affect driving skills in the same way as alcohol. Depressant drugs such as cannabis can slow down the user's reactions. Stimulant drugs such as cocaine and Ecstasy can make people feel they are in control of a car even though they are driving dangerously. The police can use a saliva test and urine or blood samples to test for drugs.

In focus: drugs in sport

Drugs are sometimes used illegally to improve performance in sport. Some are stimulants which are taken to boost brain and body speed and improve reactions. Others are used to slow down the heart rate and prevent tiredness or block pain. Some can be used to bulk up body weight and increase muscle growth.

Sports leagues and competitions have strict rules against taking drugs, and carry out random testing usually through urine or blood samples. A failed drugs test can result in disqualification from a competition.

CASE STUDY

Jared began using drugs at the age of 13, when a friend offered him some cannabis. Jared was soon smoking cannabis daily, sometimes several joints a day. Smoking pot relaxed him and made him feel good. When a friend offered him heroin at a party, Jared couldn't resist. After three hits of heroin, he was hooked. But he soon found he needed to use more of the drug to get the same high. As his habit spiralled out of control, so did the cost. Jared started stealing money from his mother and brother. When he still needed more to pay for the drugs, Jared turned to shoplifting CDs and watches and then selling the stolen goods. He knew he was taking risks, but his whole life began to revolve around his next fix of heroin. Eventually, Jared stole credit cards so that he could buy products and sell them on the street for cash. He was caught, convicted, and sent to prison.

Chapter 7: *Getting help*

Many people who smoke want to give up. Some try, but reach for a cigarette again when they are under stress. However, millions of people each year do manage to quit. Help is available to people who want to stop smoking, through their family doctor, pharmacists, telephone helplines and therapists.

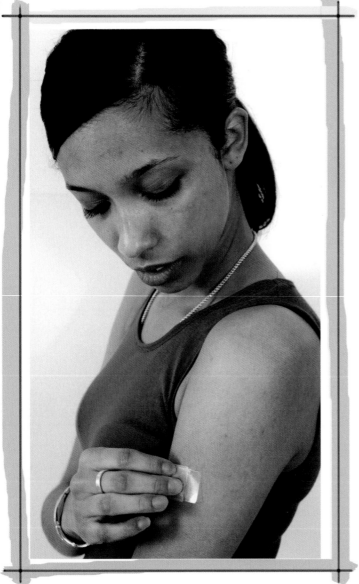

Making a plan

The first step in stopping smoking is to want to quit. It helps to make a list of all the benefits of quitting, such as having fewer coughs and chest infections, feeling better and fitter, having more money to spend on other things, having cleaner, fresher clothes and reducing the risk of smoking-related diseases.

It can be useful if people rethink their attitude towards smoking and forcefully adopt the view that "nothing is made better if I have a cigarette". It helps if people set a date on which to stop smoking and ask their friends and family for support. Planning a reward for each milestone without cigarettes,

Nicotine patches release small amounts of the drug into the skin to wean smokers off their cravings.

a day, a week, a month and so on, is useful too. It is also a good idea to save the money that would have been spent on cigarettes and put it towards special treats or rewards.

Taking action

Smoking is a habit. People who want to stop smoking should try to avoid the people that might tempt them to smoke. It helps to hang out with friends who don't smoke and to go to places where smoking is not allowed.

People who find they miss the physical sensation of a cigarette in their mouth or hands can try using dummy cigarettes, chewing sugar-free gum or snacking on something healthy when they have cravings. If they get a strong craving, experts advise them to take slow, deep breaths and delay reaching for a cigarette. The nicotine craving may pass if they can hold out for a few minutes.

Nicotine replacement therapy

Some people find that they need help to overcome nicotine cravings. Nicotine replacement therapy includes skin patches and gel, micro-tabs (tablets) nasal sprays, gum and lozenges.

These work by giving small amounts of nicotine to curb cravings. Skin patches come in different strengths that can be reduced as the cravings lessen. Some people like to use nicotine inhalators because these replace the feeling of holding and inhaling cigarettes.

New therapies

Scientists are constantly looking for new ways to help people stop smoking. They have developed pills that reduce cravings and withdrawal symptoms by making the taste of cigarettes less pleasant. Other therapies that are used to help people quit smoking include hypnotherapy, acupuncture and **cognitive behavioural therapy** (CBT).

In focus: withdrawal symptoms

Nicotine is as addictive as heroin or cocaine, and is one of the most poisonous drugs in its concentrated form. When people stop smoking they have to overcome withdrawal symptoms which can include dizziness, depression, irritability, sleep problems, headaches and an increased appetite. Symptoms usually start within a few hours of the last cigarette and peak two or three days later. They can last anything from a few days to several weeks.

Drug treatment

It can be hard for someone to give up drugs once they have become addicted. Even when someone stops taking an addictive drug, fatty tissues in the body can continue to release residues of drugs into the bloodstream, causing mental and physical cravings. Some people do manage to give up drugs on their own, but others need support.

The first step is for drug users to accept that they have a problem and be able to confide in someone they trust. It is important that they feel supported through withdrawal, as this will increase their chances of staying off the drugs. As drugs carry many health risks and effects, a person wanting to give up drugs should see a family doctor who can carry out a health check. Some doctors may be able to offer treatment for addiction at their own surgeries, but many refer patients to specialist clinics where they can be assessed and given treatment for their addiction.

Counselling therapies

Some people may find one-to-one counselling helpful in understanding why they started taking drugs and became addicted. It may also help them devise other ways of coping with the pressures that made them turn to drugs in the first place. Group therapy may also help. Drug users who are taking part in group therapy meet together to discuss their problems and find ways of helping each other through withdrawal.

Supportive one-to-one counselling can be vital in helping drug users to overcome any setbacks they may encounter in their efforts to give up drugs.

Fitness training can be an important part of rehab schemes. They help to improve both physical health and feelings of well-being.

Substitute drugs

In some cases, doctors may prescribe substitute medication to help wean someone off addictive drugs. These drugs may reduce cravings, block the effects of the drug, or give it unpleasant side effects. **Methadone** may be prescribed for heroin addicts to prevent cravings and withdrawal, but can itself be highly addictive, and there are cases of addicts who go on taking heroin with methadone, or who sell on their methadone to others.

Staying clean

When people are trying to stay off drugs, it helps them to keep busy and distracted. Boredom and depression can both lead to relapse. They should try to avoid people or places that might tempt them back into taking drugs.

In focus: rehab clinics

Some entertainment stars have attended drug rehabilitation, or rehab, clinics to help them overcome addiction. Such clinics offer patients medical supervision through the period of withdrawal. Addicts go through a programme of physical detoxification ("detox") to cleanse their body of drugs by taking a reduced amount each day. They may also be given an exercise programme to follow. Counselling and other therapies can help people find out what led to their drug dependency. Some patients stay in rehab for up to six months and may go on to live in supported housing, where counsellors are available to help them stay drug-free.

Alcohol addiction

The first step in overcoming alcohol addiction is for someone to admit that they have a problem. Many people who are alcoholics tell themselves and others that they can stop drinking if they want to. But if alcoholics try to stop drinking, they will experience strong cravings and unpleasant withdrawal symptoms that can include shakes, tremors, anxiety and sleeping problems. Most alcoholics will need help to stop drinking.

Seeking treatment

Most people who seek treatment for alcohol addiction start by going to see their family doctor or by joining a self-help group for alcoholics. Doctors can give advice on managing alcohol addiction and can refer patients for counselling or other therapies. Some people will have counselling with an alcohol specialist. Others may need a combination of treatments including talking and drug therapies. Talking therapies, such as one to one counselling or self-help groups, are important. This is because people who have abused alcohol may find it useful to identify the underlying problems that have led to their addiction, and may want help in devising new ways of coping.

Detox and rehab

Alcohol addicts need to go through detoxification first to get rid of the alcohol in their bodies. Detox programmes can be carried out at home with the support of doctors, nurses or social workers. They can also take place in a hospital or a residential clinic. Recovering addicts then go through a rehabilitation programme to help them stay off drinking (see page 39). Live-in clinics have become famous for treating celebrities with alcohol problems, but most people receive treatment at home.

Some people may need others to encourage them to admit to their problems and seek help to overcome them.

Drug therapies

Tranquillizers or beta-blockers may be given to help patients relax and get through withdrawal symptoms. Other drugs work by blocking cravings or by making people feel very sick if they drink alcohol while they are taking the drugs.

Liver damage

If an alcoholic has cirrhosis, he or she may need a liver transplant. However, if an alcoholic were to begin drinking again after a transplant, damage would recur. In order to help prevent this, surgeons can fit an implant under the fat around the stomach that releases drugs into the bloodstream to discourage the patient from drinking

alcohol again. The drugs stop the body breaking the alcohol down, so toxins build up in the blood, leading to heart palpitations and sickness.

CASE STUDY

Amber started drinking when she was 14 years old. She used to hang around with her friends, drinking beer or vodka. She was drinking so much, it affected her schoolwork and she failed her exams. This just made her rely on alcohol even more, and she soon found her day revolved around drinking. One night she drank so much vodka she collapsed with alcohol poisoning and had to be taken to hospital. Amber's family doctor referred her to a self-help group for alcoholics. Amber went twice a week. Listening to others in the group was like listening to her own story. Hearing how some had overcome their drink problems gave her hope that she could too. The group operated a buddy system through which members could give one another support when they felt they might relapse. Amber called her buddy whenever she was tempted to drink. The first few weeks were the hardest, but Amber's buddy kept her focused on conquering her addiction.

Chapter 8: *Tackling the problem*

Reports from the World Health Organization (WHO) show that smoking and alcohol and drug abuse are major causes of ill health and death around the world.

Smoking

Smoking rates are increasing among women and young people, especially in Japan and developing countries. Tobacco advertisers target young people in these countries with billboards near schools and colleges, and by handing out free cigarettes at youth events. The rates for young smokers are rising in China, Japan, Africa and the Middle East.

Alcohol abuse

Alcohol abuse is rising in Europe, Russia and many developing countries. One in four deaths of young men is

A sign in this Hong Kong restaurant reminds customers of the ban on smoking in public places which is in place – and warns of the penalty for flouting it.

due to alcohol, and in Europe alone around 50,000 young people die from drink related causes each year. In Russia, one in three men and one in seven women are addicted to alcohol. Russia has seen a rise in deaths from alcohol poisoning, often the result of drinking illicit 'moonshine' (homemade vodka) or household products such as cleaning fluids and aftershaves. WHO estimates that alcohol abuse causes between 20 and 30 per cent of murders and traffic accidents worldwide each year.

Drugs

In parts of Europe, Africa, Asia and the United States, abuse of prescription drugs is now overtaking abuse of recreational drugs such as heroin, cocaine and Ecstasy. In the United States, it is second only to cannabis use. There is widespread online trafficking of prescription drugs, and they are also easily available through online pharmacies, many of which sell controlled drugs without prescription.

Global action

The World Health Organization has called for wider bans on tobacco and alcohol advertising, promotion and sponsorship. There are also calls for more bans on smoking in public places and higher taxes on tobacco and alcohol

It's a fact:
fatal habits

- According to the World Health Organization, smoking and alcohol each account for 4 per cent of the global burden of disease.
- Alcohol abuse causes nearly two million deaths each year and one in ten cases of illness and disease in Europe.
- Smoking kills around five million people a year; in 2020 this figure is predicted to rise to ten million, with 70 per cent of deaths in developing countries.
- Illicit drug abuse accounts for 0.8 per cent of the global burden of ill health.

to reduce consumption. New laws may be needed to prevent online drug trafficking and to control the sale of prescription drugs on the Internet. Another strategy is introducing more education programmes in schools, colleges and youth clubs, to inform young people about the risks of smoking and drug and alcohol abuse.

It's your health

Sometimes when you are growing up you feel as if you want to try everything out. When people tell you something is bad for you, it has little impact. You feel young and healthy; you are not ready to think or worry about illness and old age. You may know about people who use alcohol, tobacco and drugs and live to a good age. You may hear stories of teens who died after taking drugs or through alcohol poisoning, but they are the exception. It's your life isn't it, and your decision what you do with it?

But sometimes when we think we are making our own decisions, we are really being influenced by others – whether friends, celebrities or advertisers. Saying no to what others are doing is harder than going along with the crowd. It is your decision how you look after yourself and your health. Your genes can affect your health, but you can increase or reduce

There are so many ways to have fun when you are young, and keep yourself fit and on form.

It's your body and it's up to you to eat the sort of foods that keep it working well and able to fight off illnesses.

Staying healthy

Eating a healthy diet, exercising and drinking in moderation help your body stay fit and healthy. Exercise and sport increase levels of serotonin in the brain, and produce endorphins that lift your mood and make you feel good.

A diet containing plenty of fresh fruit and vegetables boosts your well-being. Some foods can even be mood-enhancers. Bananas contain tryptophan, a type of protein that the body turns into serotonin, and dark chocolate contains 'feel good' chemicals. You can change the way your body and brain work in many positive ways, without using drugs or alcohol.

health risks by what you do and how you behave. Smoking and abusing drugs or alcohol put your body under attack. If you use cigarettes or alcohol as a social prop, you need to think about why you need them. If you take drugs to escape from what is going on in your life, you need to think about what is making you unhappy or stressed, and if there is any way you can make that better.

In focus: taking action

If you have a problem with smoking, alcohol or drugs or if you know someone who has – take action now. Talk to someone you know and trust and tell them your concerns.

There are plenty of organizations that can offer help and support for addiction. Turn to page 47 for a list of organizations and people to contact.

Glossary

addiction Dependency on something to the extent that it becomes the most important thing in life, even when it causes serious medical or other consequences.

alcohol abuse Drinking alcohol so as to harm health.

alcohol poisoning A condition in which a person has consumed a toxic amount of alcohol.

alco pops Ready-mixed alcoholic drinks.

altitude sickness A disorder which people can experience while at high altitudes.

Alzheimer's A disease of the brain by which intellectual functions such as memory and reasoning progressively deteriorate.

amphetamines A group of stimulant drugs.

anabolic steroids Drugs used to increase weight and muscle growth.

barbiturates A group of depressant drugs.

binge drinking Drinking more than five alcoholic drinks in a short space of time.

blood alcohol concentration The amount of alcohol in the blood.

cilia Tiny hair-like structures.

cirrhosis A disease of the liver which causes it to become irreversibly scarred.

cognitive behavioural therapy A form of treatment for a range of mental disorders which helps patients to examine why they think and behave as they do.

coma A long period of unconsciousness.

date rape The rape of a person by someone they have met socially.

dependency Needing something so much that you cannot survive without it.

depressants Substances that slow down the nervous system.

dopamine Brain chemical associated with reward or pleasure.

drug abuse Taking illegal drugs or using prescription drugs illegally in ways that harm health.

endorphins 'Feel good' chemicals in the brain.

enzyme A type of protein that speeds up chemical reactions in the body.

euphoria A state of intense pleasure.

foetal alcohol syndrome Foetal disablement caused by a mother drinking alcohol during pregnancy.

gene The unit of heredity – how characteristics pass from parent to child.

hallucinogens Substances that produce distorted dreams or visions.

inhalants Substances breathed in through the nose or mouth.

injest To take into the body.

khat A green-leafed plant chewed as a stimulant in Africa and the Middle East.

larynx A structure at the top of the windpipe.

membrane Soft tissue lining in the body.

metabolism Chemical processes that help the body produce energy.

methadone A drug that is used to relieve pain, or as a substitute for heroin in heroin addiction programmes.

nitrites Chemicals that have an effect on the central nervous system.

obesity Having excessive body fat.

osteoporosis A decrease in bone density.

paranoia A mental disorder which makes someone think everyone is against them.

peer pressure The influence of people of the same age on a person's behaviour.

psychosis A serious mental disorder.

receptors Docking parts in or on cells that bind with chemical substances.

schizophrenia A serious mental disorder which makes it difficult for someone to tell what is real or unreal.

sedatives A group of depressant drugs.

serotonin A brain chemical associated with pleasure.

stimulants Substances that increase activity in the nervous system.

solvents Liquid substances such as glues, paints and sprays.

tolerance Gradual adaptation to the effects of something.

withdrawal The act of coming off drugs.

Further information

Books to read

Julian Cohan, *Drugs: Life Files*
(Evans Brothers 2000)
Magdalena Alagna, *Everything You Need to Know about the Dangers of Binge Drinking*
(Rosen Publishing Group 2001)
Smoking 101: An Overview for Teens
(Lerner Publications Co 2006)
Teen Alcoholism (Contemporary Times Companions)
(Greenhaven Press 2001)
Teen Smoking and Tobacco Use: A Hot Issue
(Enslan Publishers 2000)

Telephone helplines

ChildLine
A free helpline that young people in the UK can call to talk about any problems.
Telephone helpline: 0800 1111
Website address: **www.childline.org.uk/**

National smoking helpline
A free helpline run by the NHS in the UK, offering advice and support to anyone who wants to give up smoking.
Telephone helpline: 0800 169 9169

National Drugs Helpline
A free and confidential helpline which is available 24 hours a day, seven days a week in the UK. It offers information and advice to anyone who is worried about drugs, whether they are drug users themselves or they are concerned about a friend or family member who may be using drugs.
Telephone helpline: 0800 77 66 00

Helpful websites

www.talktofrank.com
The 'Talk to Frank' website offers information on drugs from A to Z. There is an opportunity for anyone who is concerned about any aspect of drug use to email counsellors via the website to ask advice. There is information for the friends and family members of drug users and the website includes stories from people describing their own experiences of drug abuse.

www.kidshealth.org/teen/drug_alcohol/ drugs/know_about_drugs.html
Part of the kids' health website aimed at teens, with lots of information on drugs and alcohol.

www.NoTobacco.org
An anti-smoking website which is aimed at teens and young people.

www.wrecked.co.uk
A website about alcohol aimed at children and teens, including a quiz, unit checker and fast facts.

www.worriedneed2talk.org.uk
A website run by the NSPCC designed to give young people information about services and people that are there to help them.

www.youngminds.org.uk
The website of a national charity that aims to improve young people's mental health.

Index

Numbers in **bold** refer to illustrations.